AF601426

Works of a consummate world-class artist, Galen Garwood's photographs are meditations and explorations that attain harmonic balance and truth in motion, infused with an astonishing awareness of color and the perpetual energy generated by dark and light. Life within these evocative works emanates from a fleeting, ceaseless center, and their vulnerability and compassion, their fearlessness and wisdom, reside within us.

~ *William O'Daly*

The DREAM SEA photographs

GALEN GARWOOD

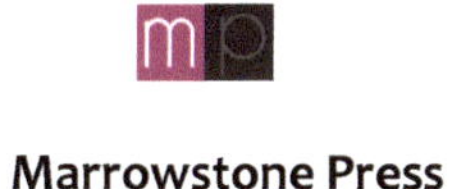

Marrowstone Press

Leave This, Away, *The Leap* (now entitled: *The Leap to Agni,*) and *Remembrance,*
published in William O'Daly's *The Road To Isla Negra*, Folded Word Press, 2015

Stephen's Dream, Akalixy Totem, The Pearls of Shiva, Raft of Pearls and *Dreaming Stone, Sleeping Star,*
published in *Water's Eye*, poems by Peter Weltner, Marrowstone Press, 2015

www.galengarwood.com

ISBN 978-0-615-66639-6

For my brothers,
Bernard, Gray, and Glenn

The DREAM SEA Photographs

The Journey Across

When I grew in the sea of my mother's womb, we were living beside the Atlantic Ocean at Folly Beach Island, near Charleston, South Carolina. I was content in those dark waters and resisted entering the world of light. I turned over and away from the portal out of which we are delivered into this world. So successful was my manoeuvre that my mother's doctor couldn't find a heartbeat. I was declared *fētus ad mortem*, and was to be eliminated within a few days. When news of my termination reached my grandmother, she swept in during the night and carried us back to Blakely, Georgia, where I was born several months later, weighing in at almost thirteen pounds. The year was 1944. I was taken back to the sea in 1949, this time to St. Simon's Island, one of the remarkable barrier islands that define the *low country* of Georgia. Here, my three older brothers and I were turned loose like young goats growing wild in the dunes on the Golden Isles, swimming in the sea, crabbing in the Marshes of Glynn, long before we could read or write, and, in general, finessing our survival instincts. Our beautiful, talented, and eccentric mother played piano and jazz organ at various night-clubs. She worked late and slept late.

For me, those were days of warmth and solitude and the sea became a treasured companion. The smells and sounds and touch of the ocean carved an indelible repository of memories out of which my dreams are still shaped. When I was taken away from the sea at age eleven, I carried with me an olfactory snapshot. Years later, sitting in a cafe in the frozen tundra of Alaska, well into my second decade, a waitress walked by and with her came the wafting smell of my childhood sea—the salty air and sweet perfume of pink oleander that grew wild on the beaches. I stopped her and asked what perfume she was wearing. "Shalimar," she said. I laughed. *Shalimar*, a garden, a temple of love, comes to us from Sanskrit. I later discovered it had been my mother's favorite perfume when I was a child growing up by the sea.

Even at 70, I still have the snapshot. I remember the smell. The cells of the brain enjoy their own constancy: death and rebirth, the endless transferring of data in near perfect replication, dying cell to new cell, such that memory and dreams do not grow old.

I now live far away from the beaches of my childhood, near a small village in Northern Thailand. Still, here in the shadows of vast bamboo groves, the sounds of a small river and the roar of the dam's water-spill in front of my studio comfort me. I smile at the wondrous weaving of it all, here and now, another life in another world. I've grown old, perhaps not truly old, not as I might come to be. There's comfort there. How easy and natural it seems to inspect the desiccating folds of my wrinkled skin with the imperturbable curiosity of a child.

I recite *Buddha's Five Remembrances*, reflecting on the inescapability of ageing, of illness, of the loss of all that is dear and especially the notion that one's only real possessions are one's actions, the consequences of which one cannot escape.

The immutableness of art is like a message placed in a bottle and tossed into the sea. It finds its way into vast oceans, something of and to the world, floating across underwater universes, over iridescent reefs. I dream it being visited by passing inhabitants—small seabirds who come and rest on the bottle's neck; curious fish and animals and floating crustaceans are enraptured by their own curved, spinning images reflected back into the sky.

The bottle becomes etched by relentless winds and particles of sands from deserts and mountains—the Great Steppes of Mongolia, the Serengeti, the Gobi, and yes, even the bright island sand of my youth—lifted by winds, then offered to the sculpting eddies of oceans. And I think of my brother Gray's beautiful ashes I long ago cast out into the Straits of Juan de Fuca with a small raft of roses. He too moved through the tides, into the mouths of small fish which in turn feed larger fish or white pelicans diving into the slate coloured water; how easy to envision my brother a bird crossing the sea, aloft in the lungs of the earth, dreaming of land—everything from one necklace of stars, exploding like jewels across the stark emptiness of stellar space.

One day shallow currents will nudge the drifting bottle onto a rocky beach, a continent away. Perhaps someone I've never met, buffeted by artic winds, will be walking along the shore, carefully treading rocks and the Bullwhip kelp that grows in great snaky masses. His eyes catch something ensnared in the tangled mound of giant sea grass. He leans over, fishes out a stoppered bottle, opaquely burnished the brown and green of oceans. With cold fingers he pries loose the cork.

A swooshing sound.

The faint scent of pink oleander escapes into the air. Quickly he twists the cork back into the bottle and turns toward home. He wonders what's inside. Imagination? Destiny? Perhaps both. Perhaps they're the same. He looks back at the sea and marvels at the mystery and weight of the bottle's journey, its texture and symmetry, its architecture and possibility.

Galen Garwood 2015

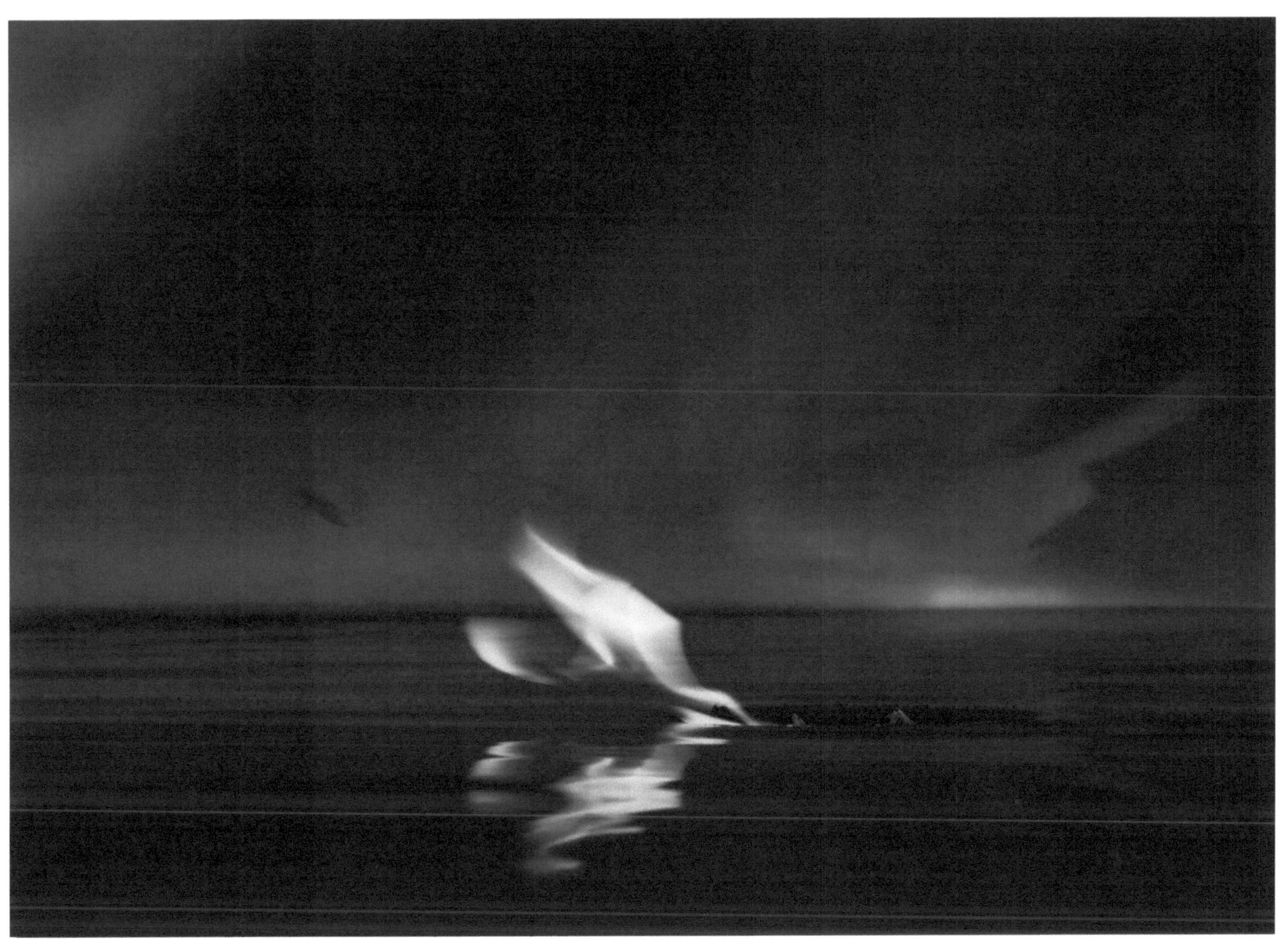

Final Flight

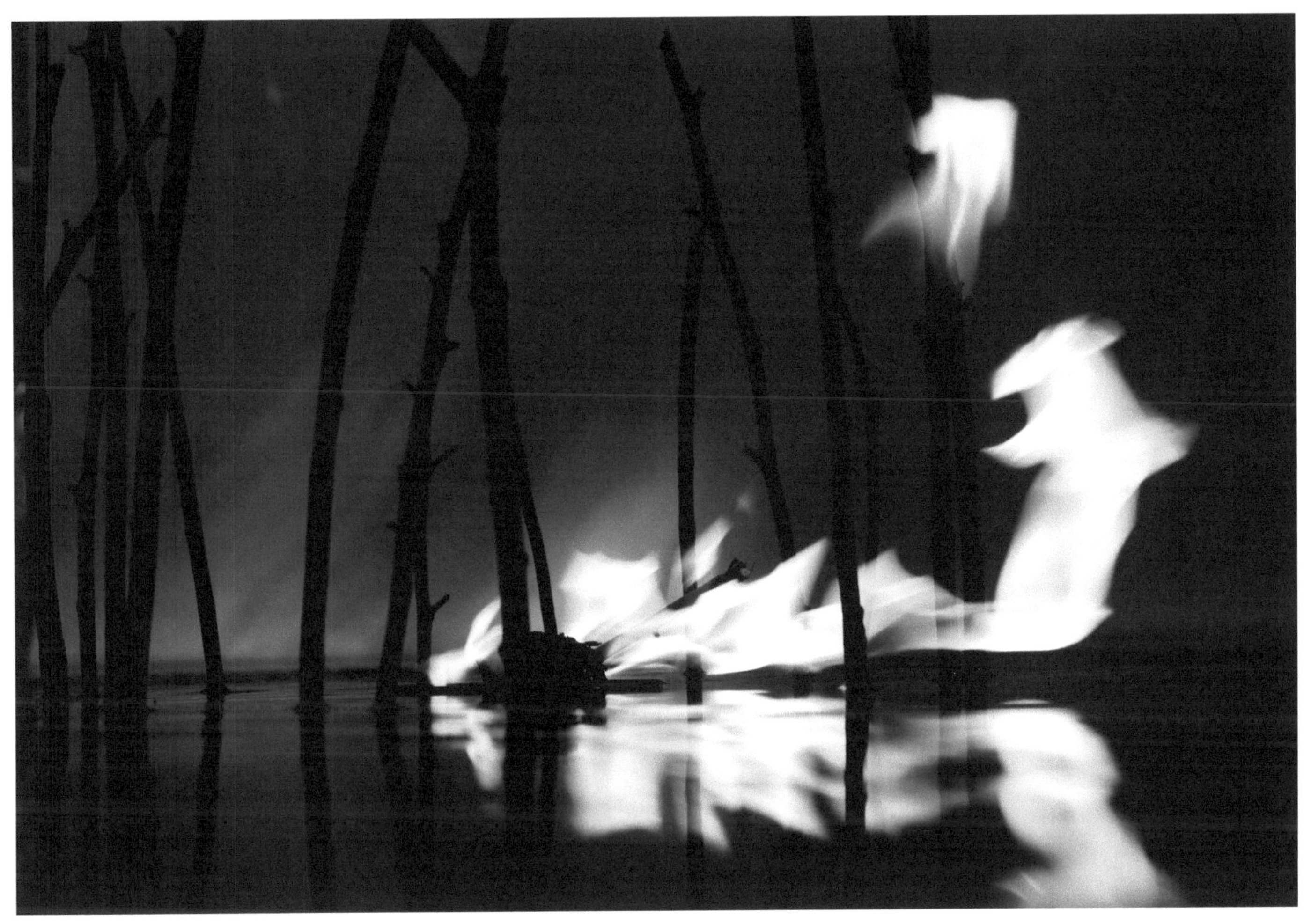

The Leap to Agni

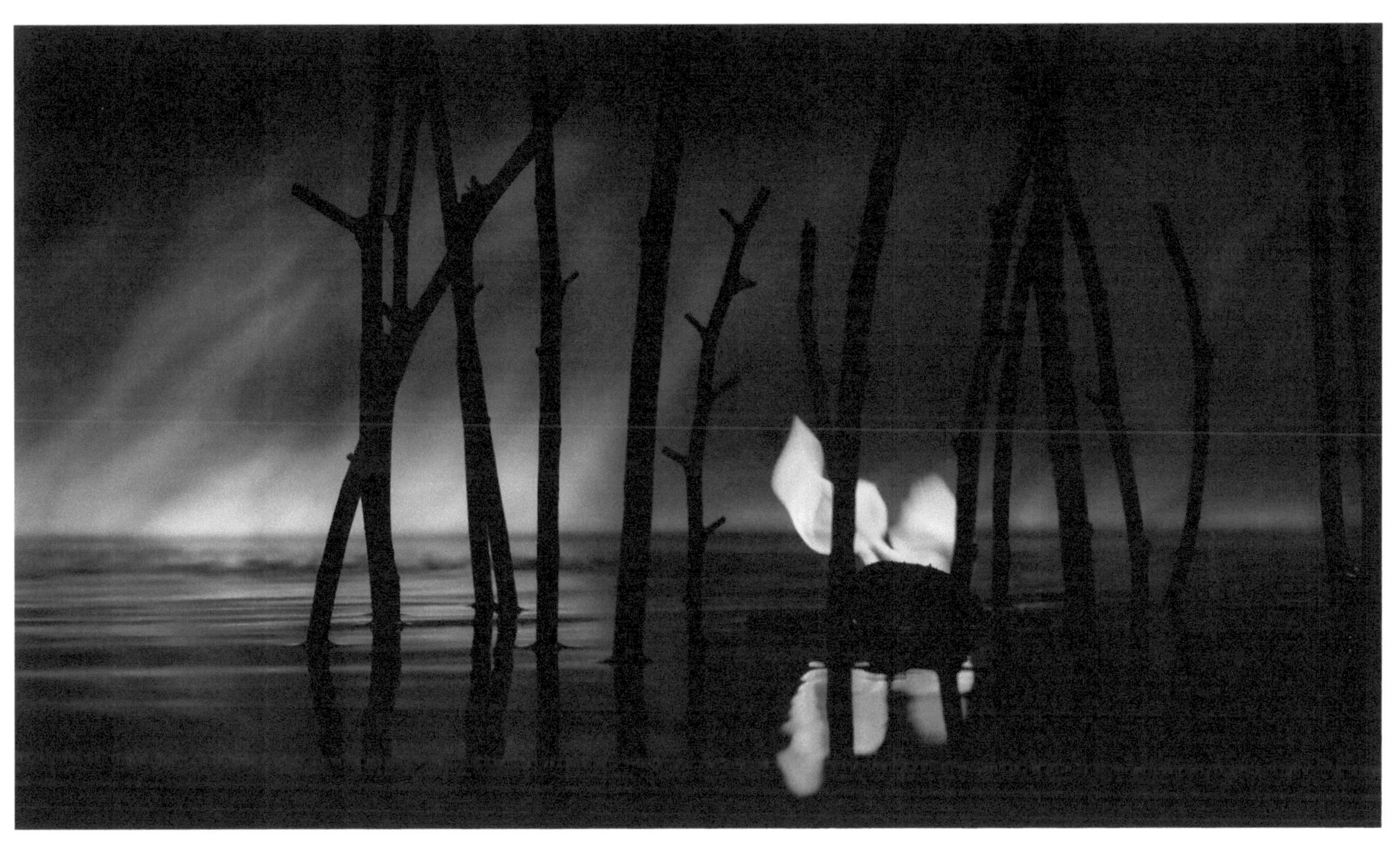

Gathering the Light

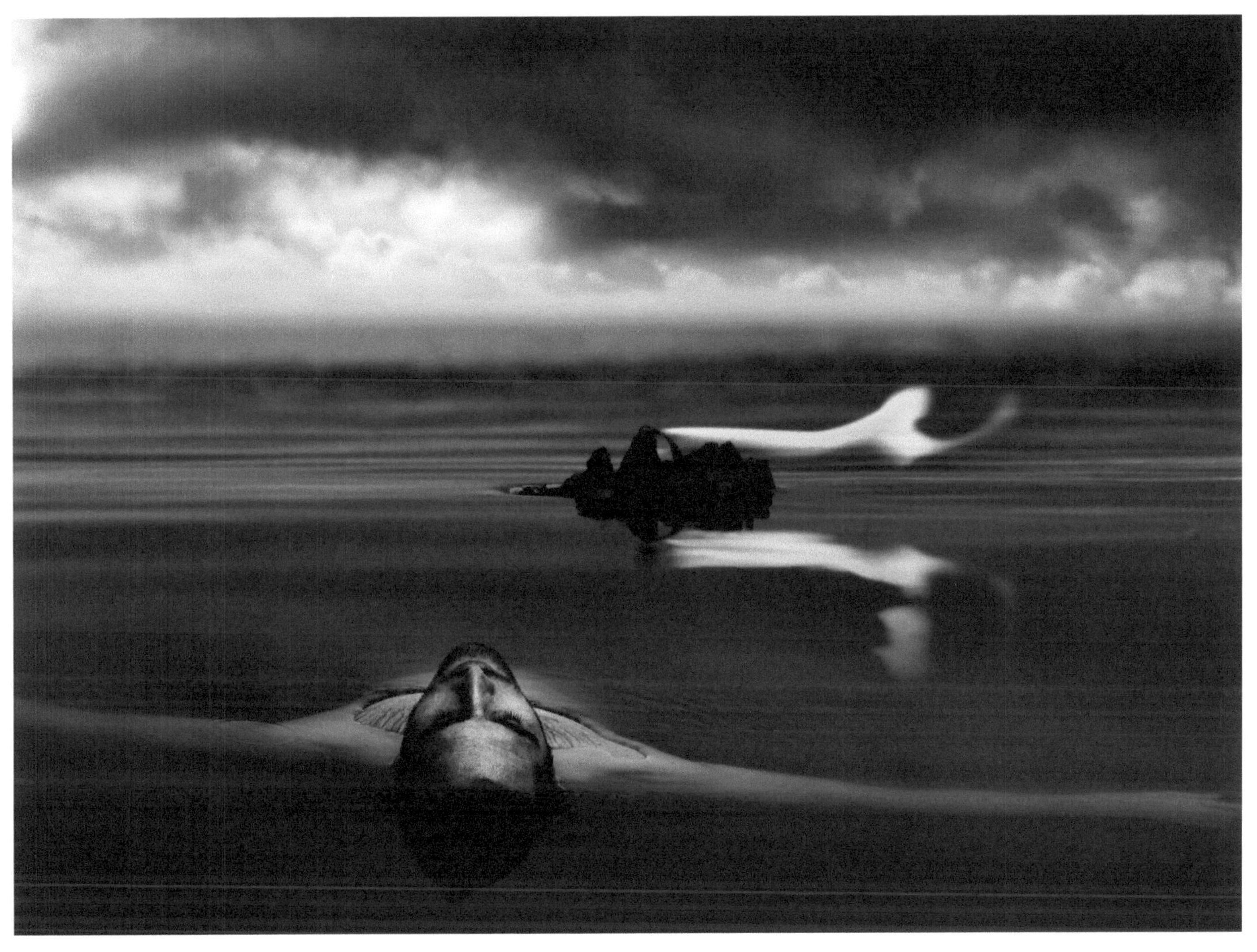

Remembrance

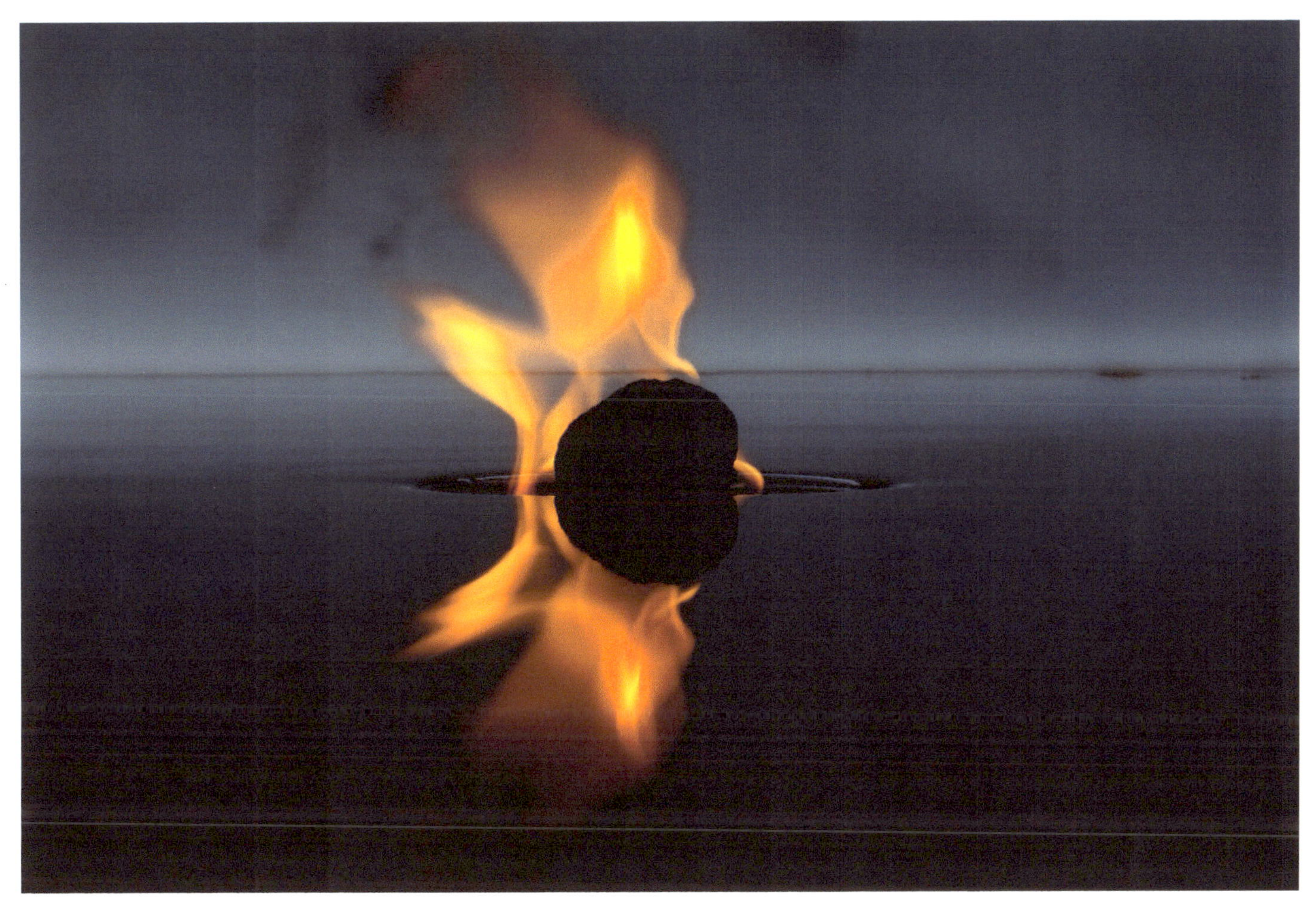

The Dream Stone

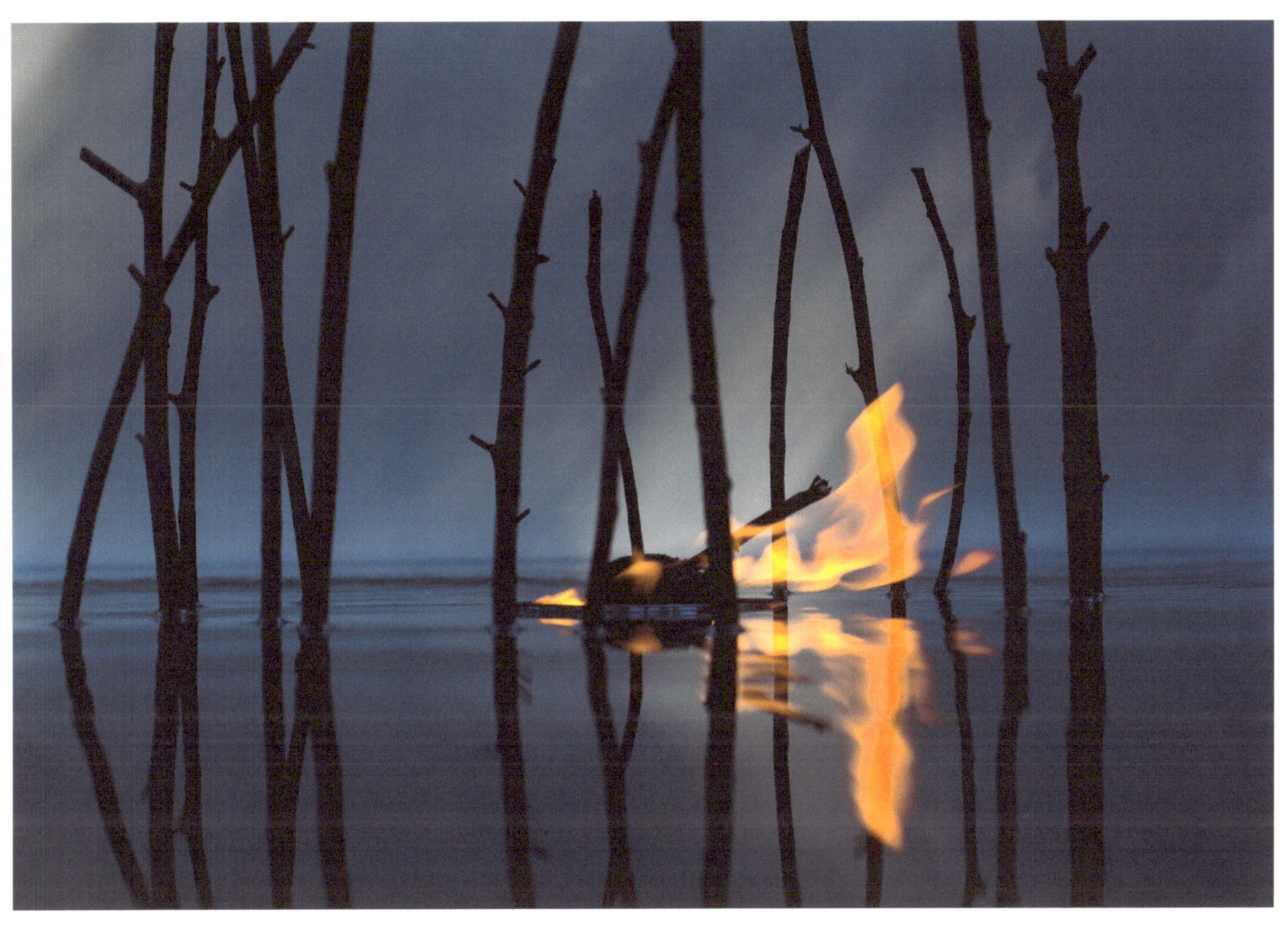

The Butterly's Dream

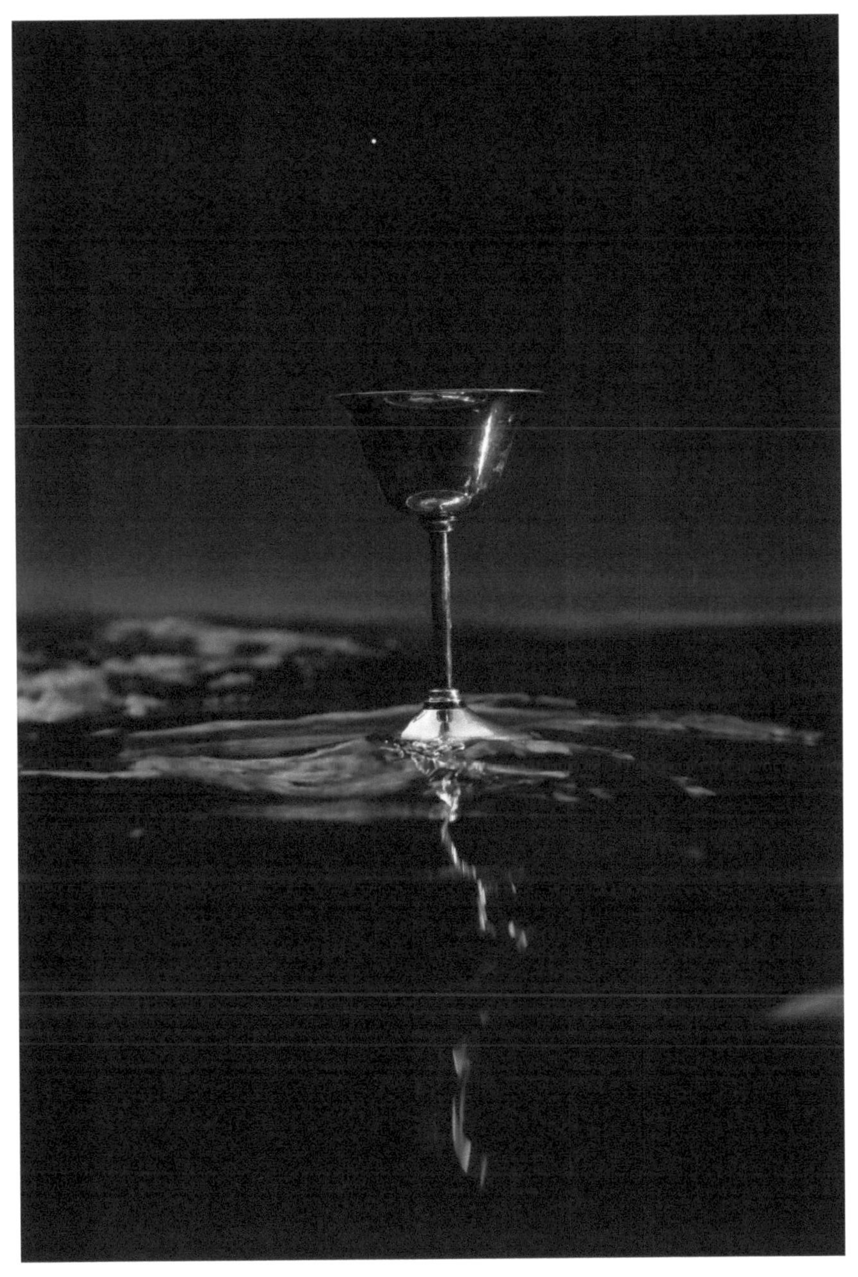

Palaimon's Chalice

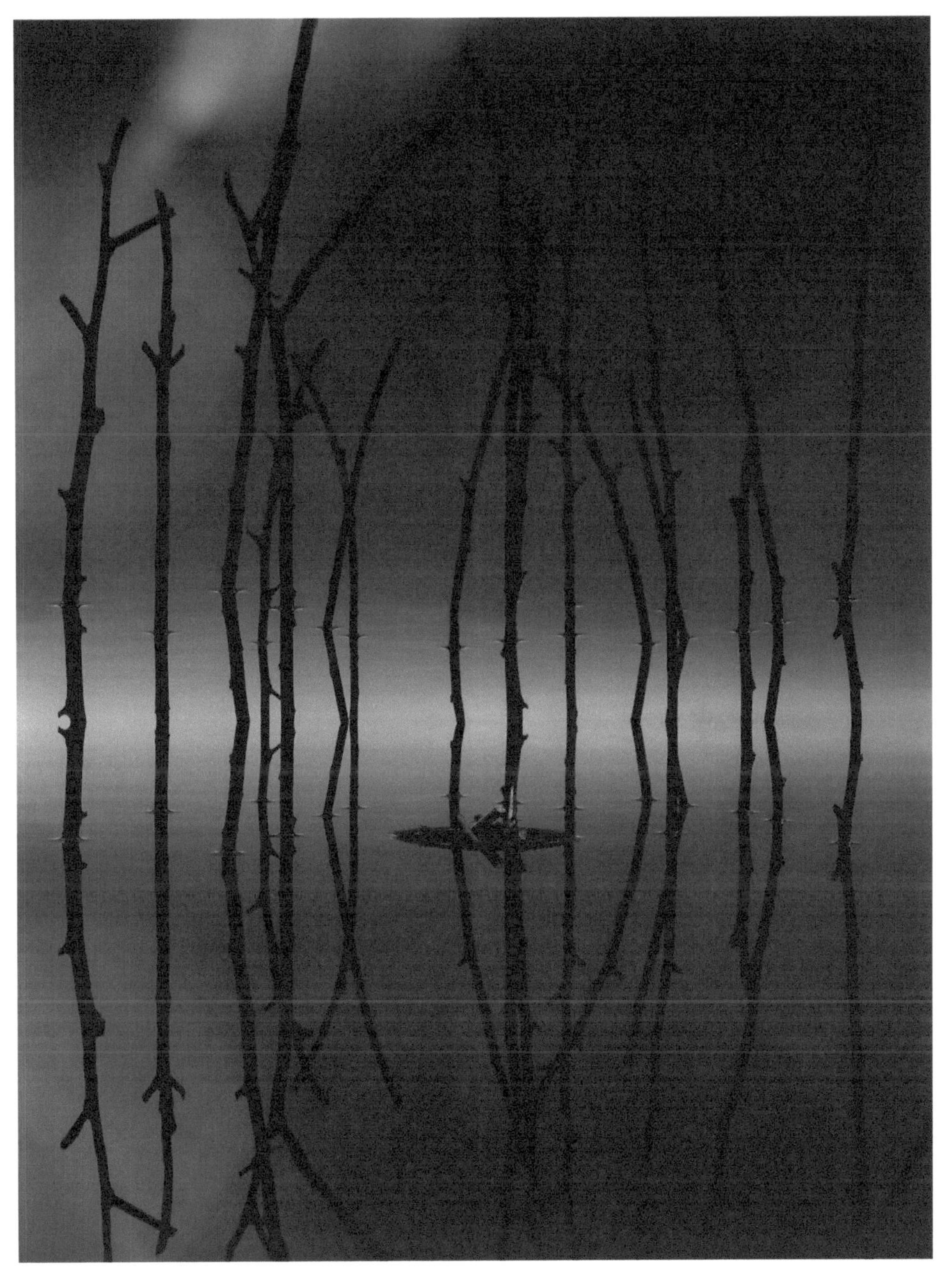

The Gathering

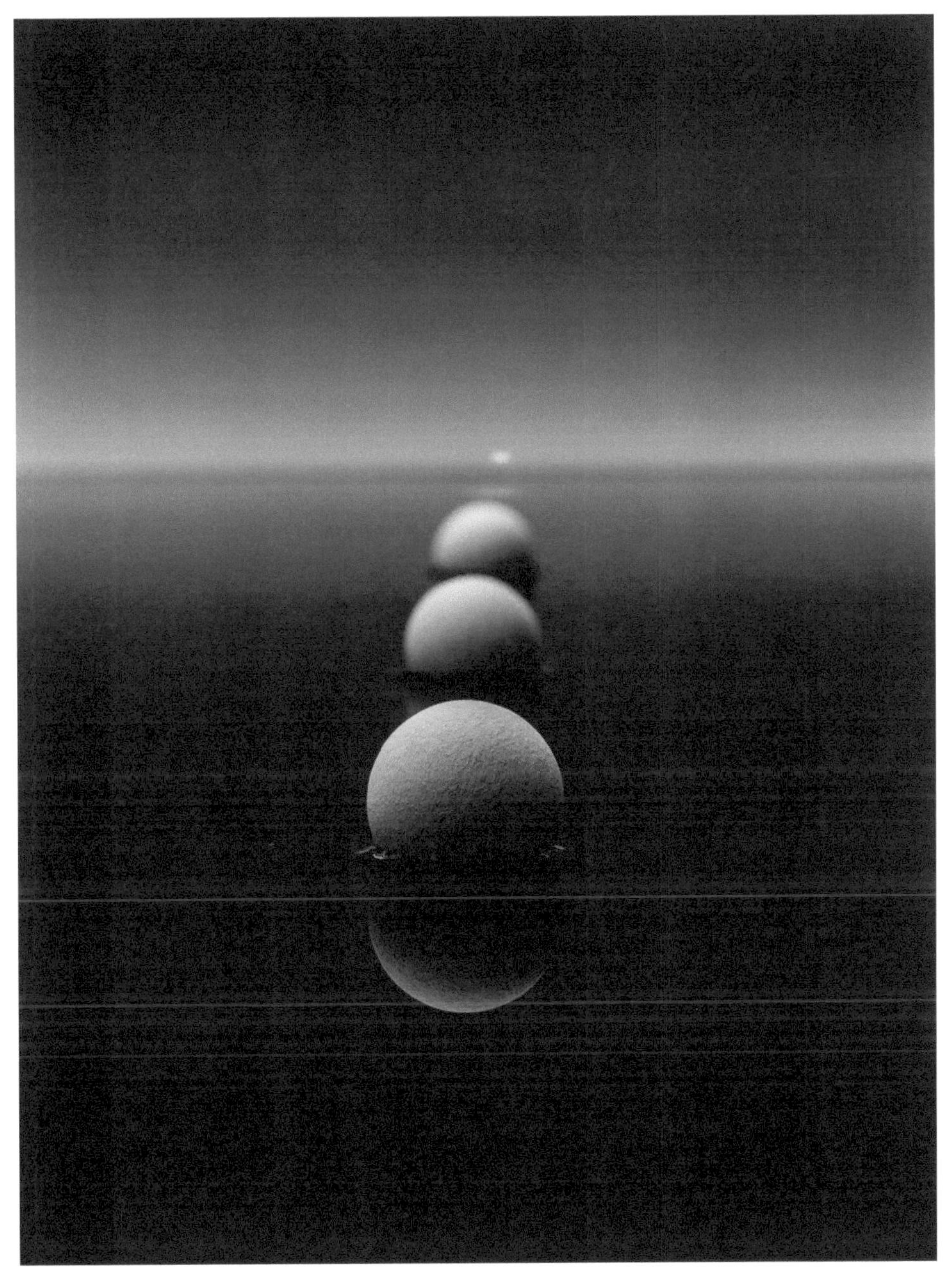

Akalixy Totem

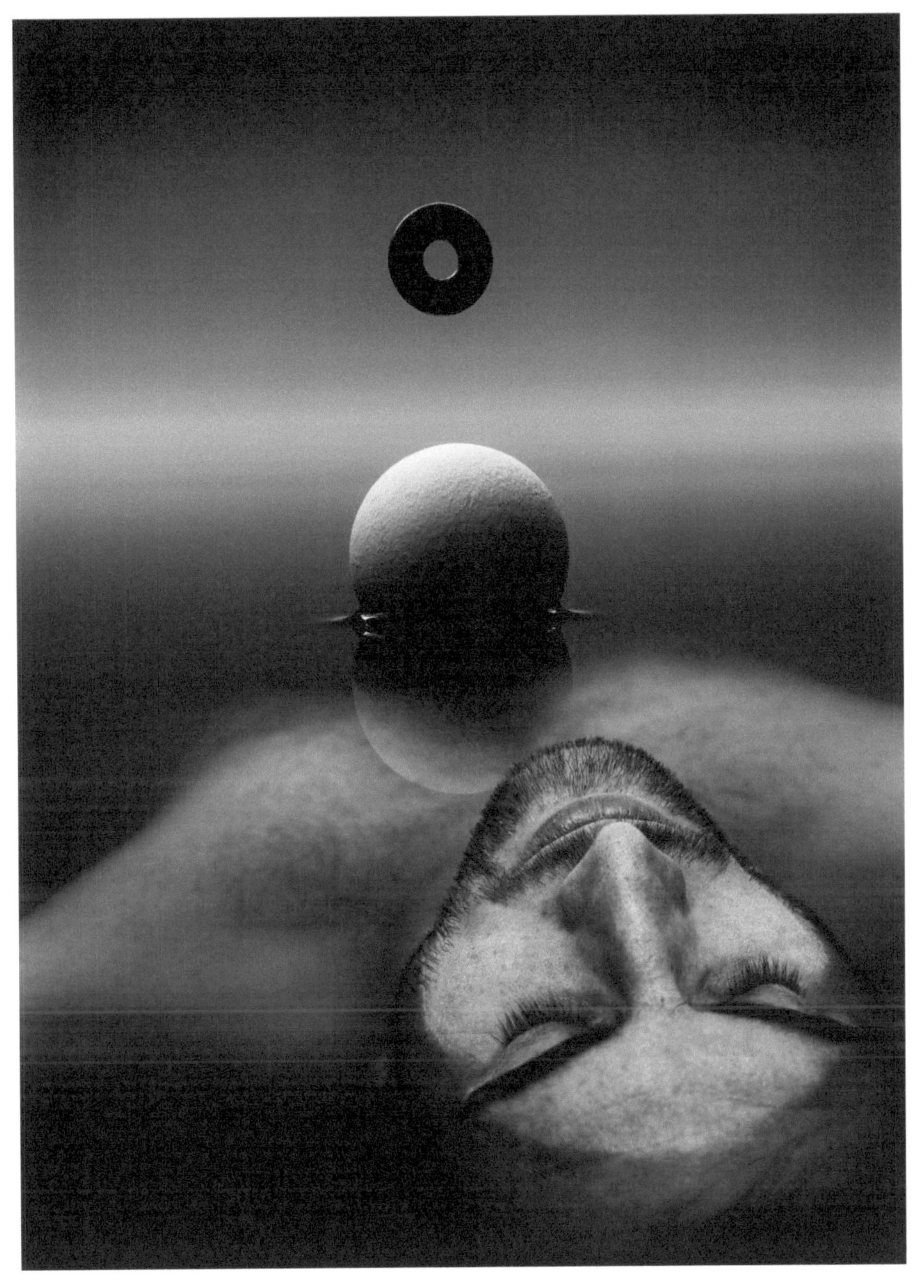

Stephen's Dream

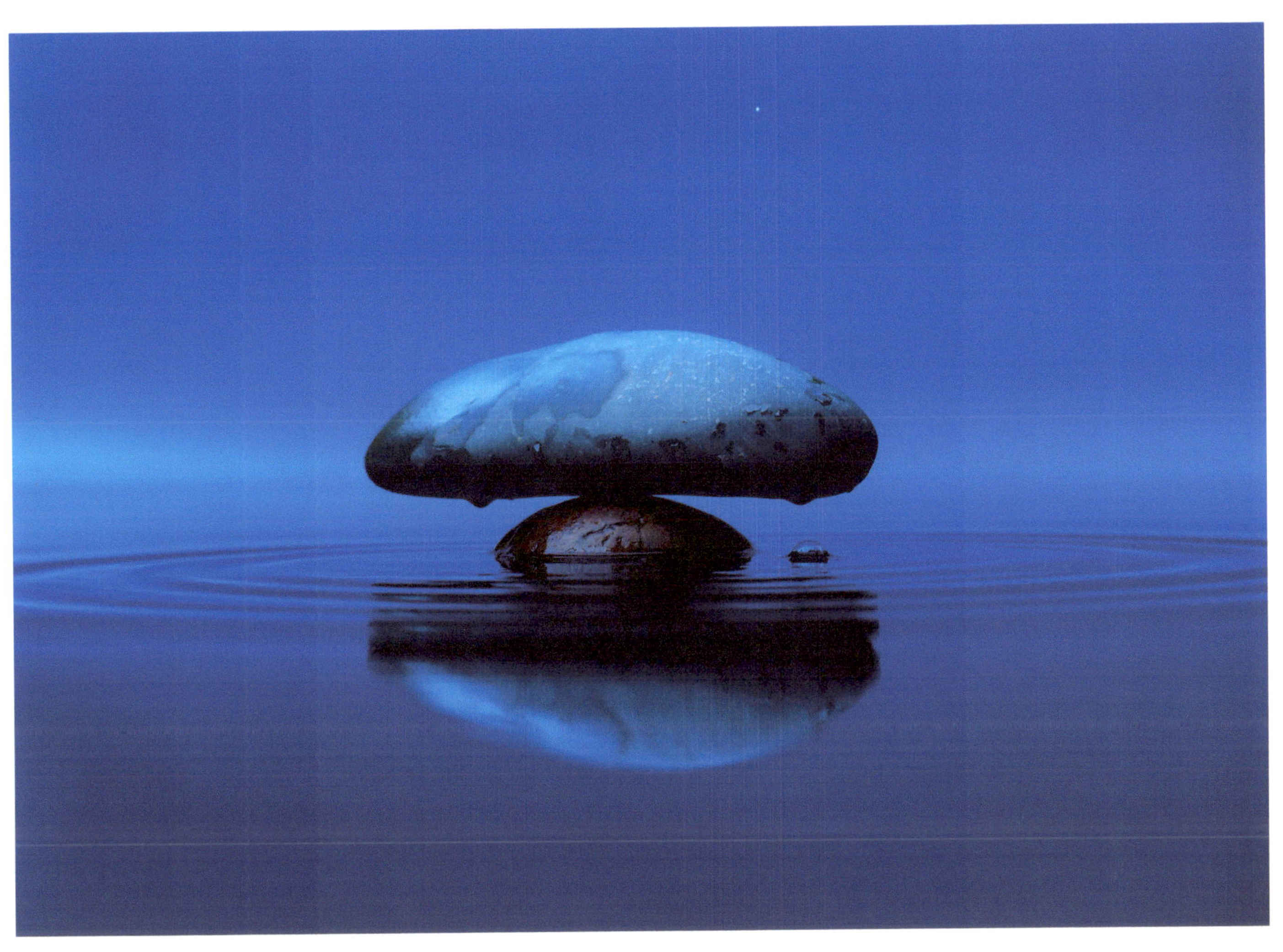

Sleeping Stone, Breathing Star

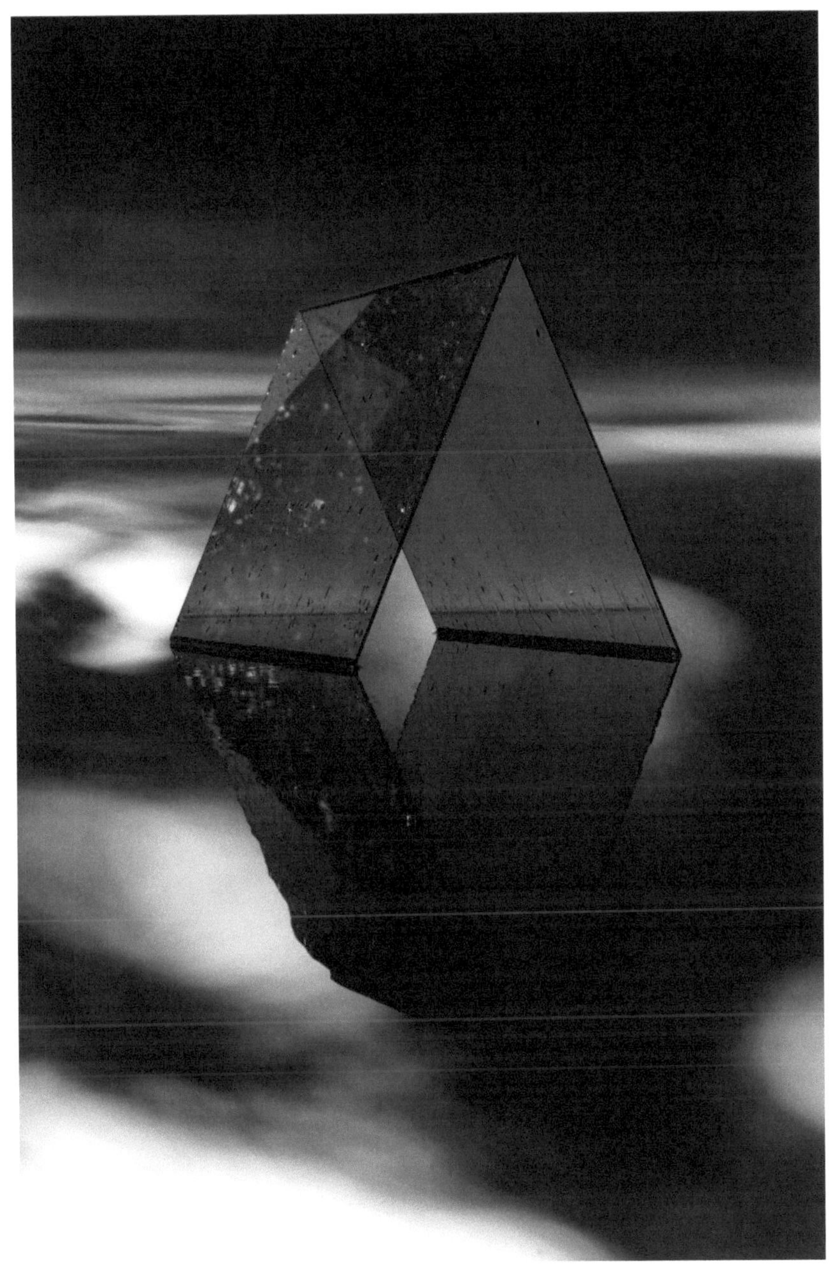

Into Swah

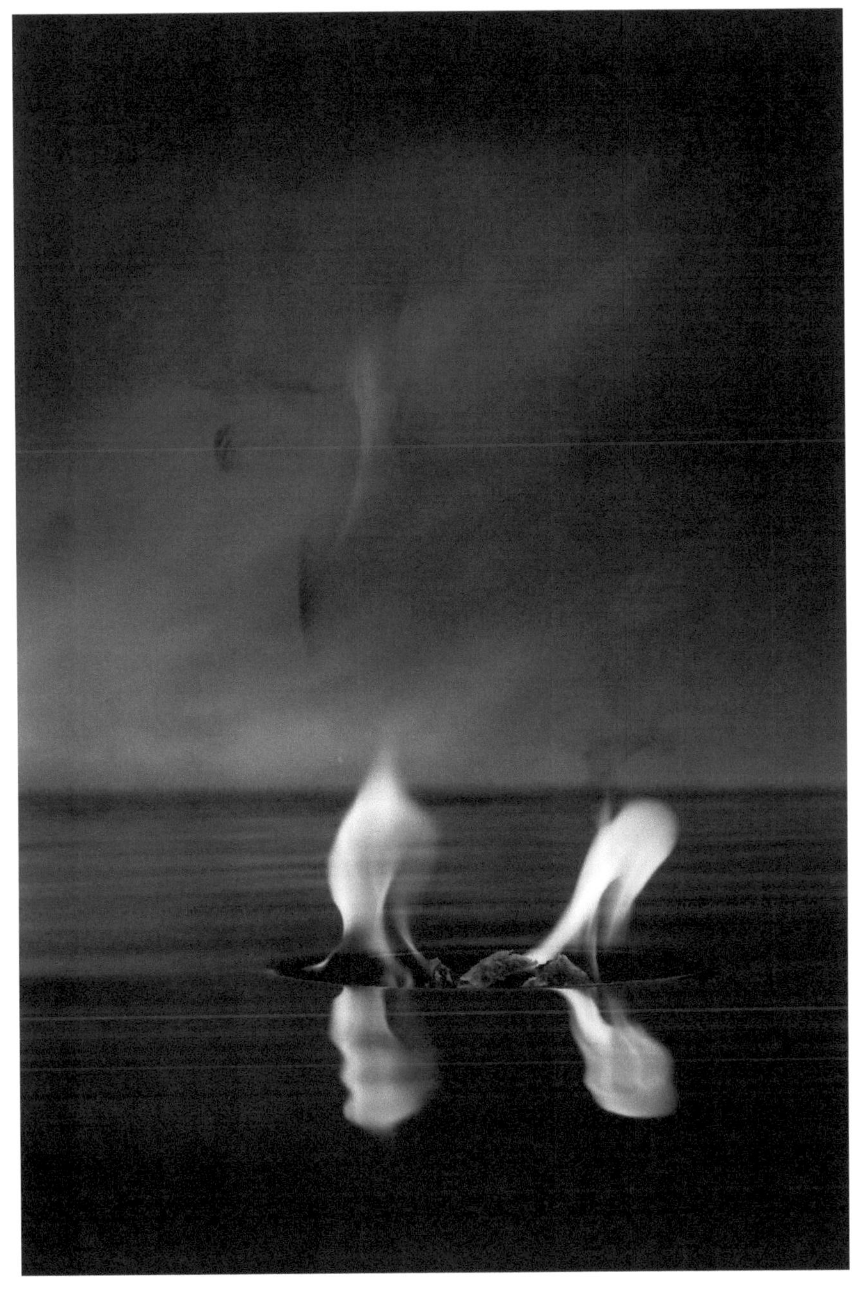

Resurrection

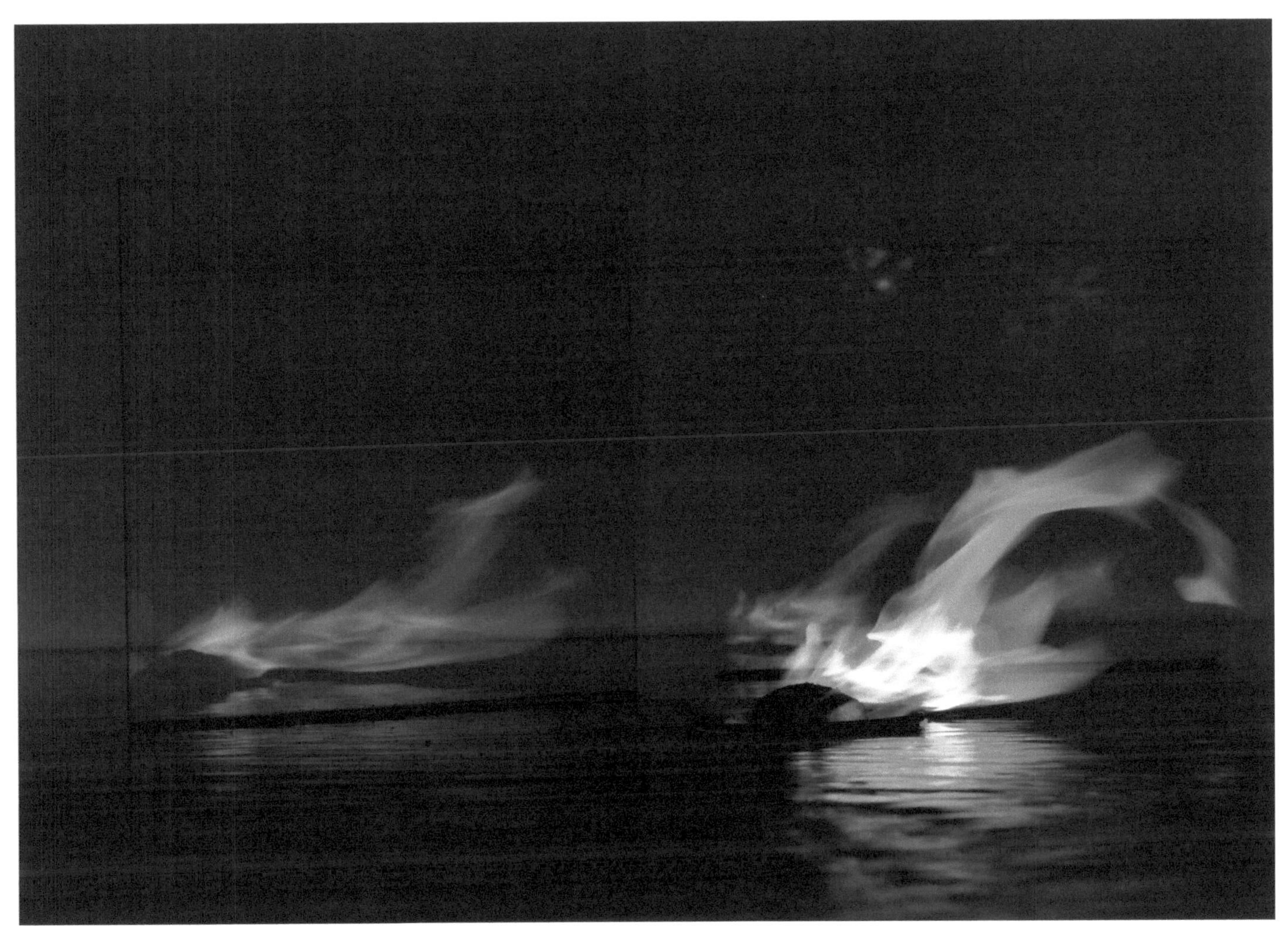

Leave This, Away

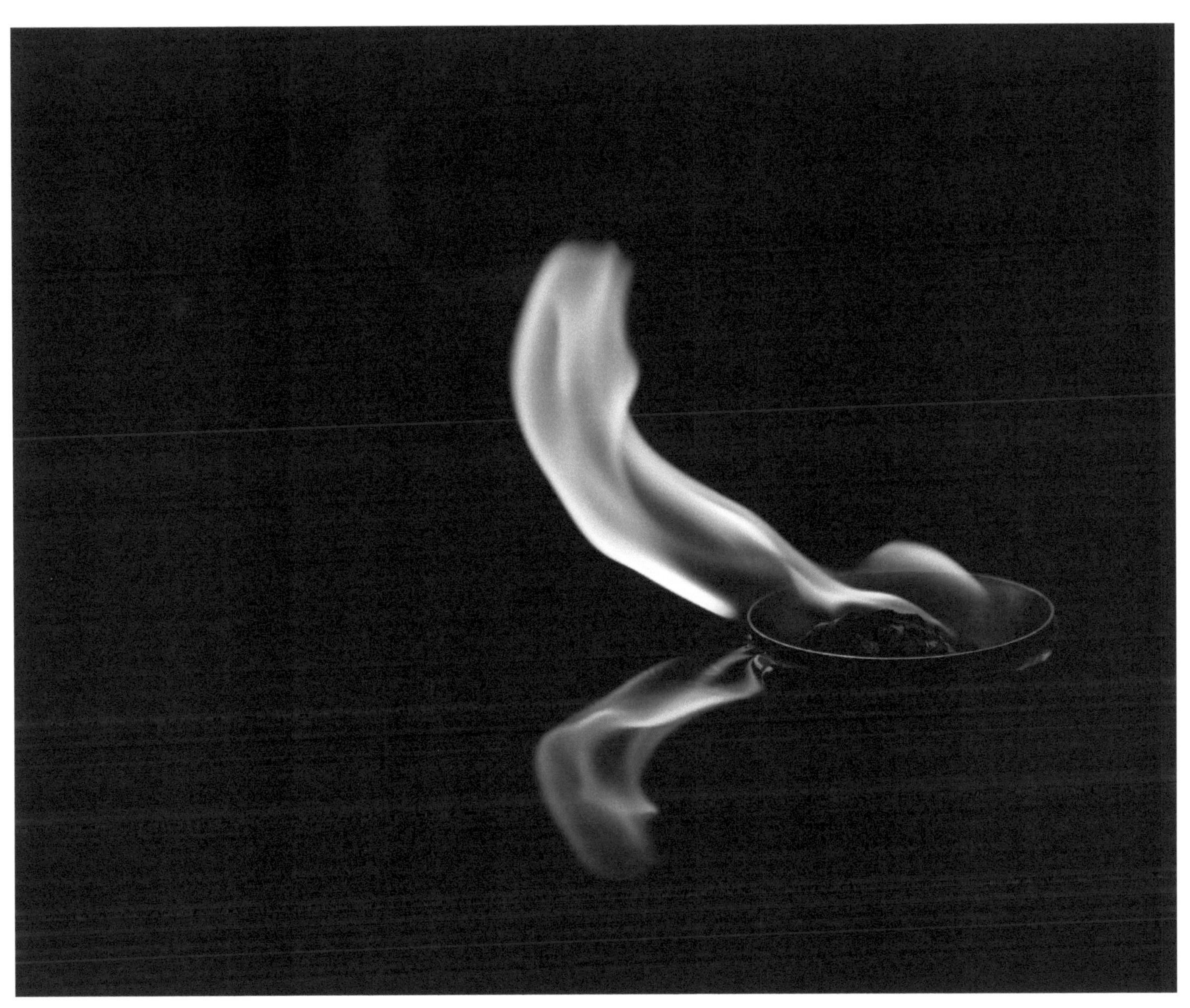

Burzn

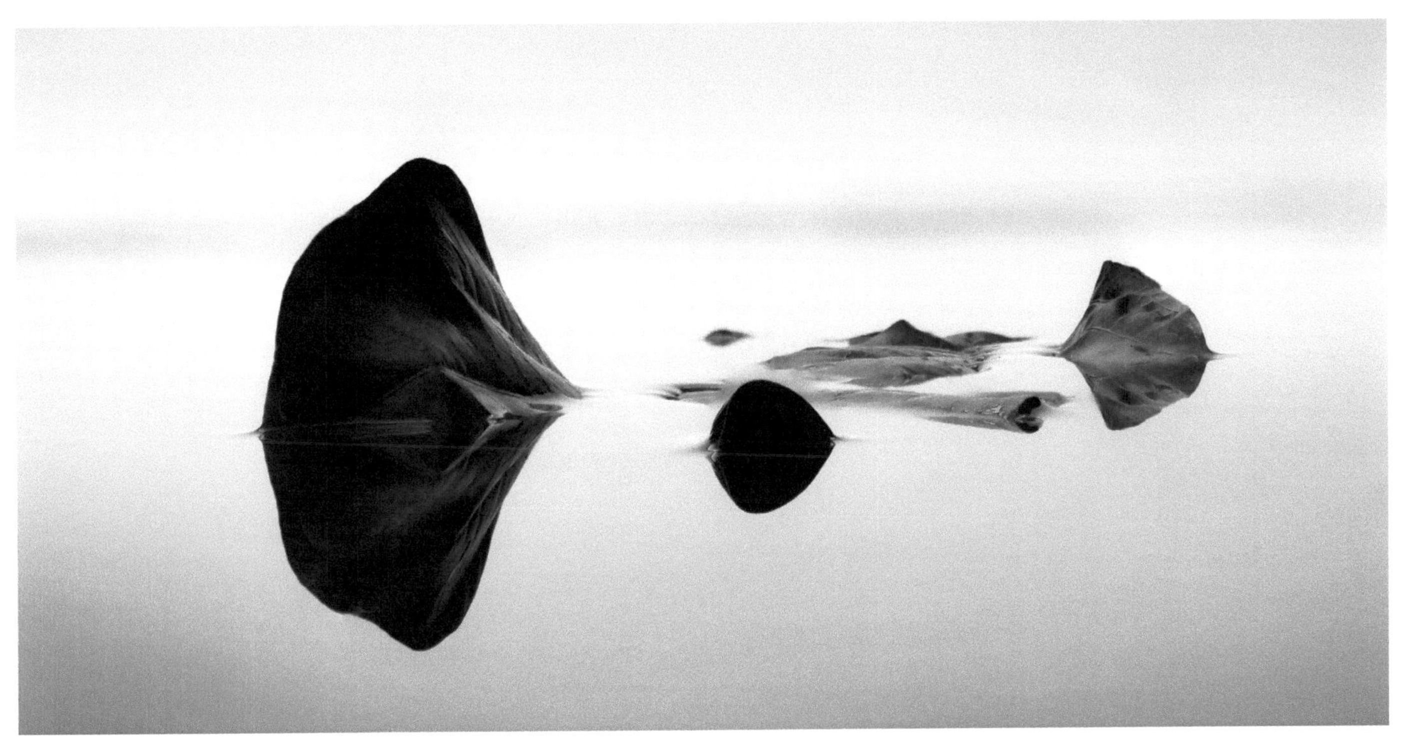

Raft

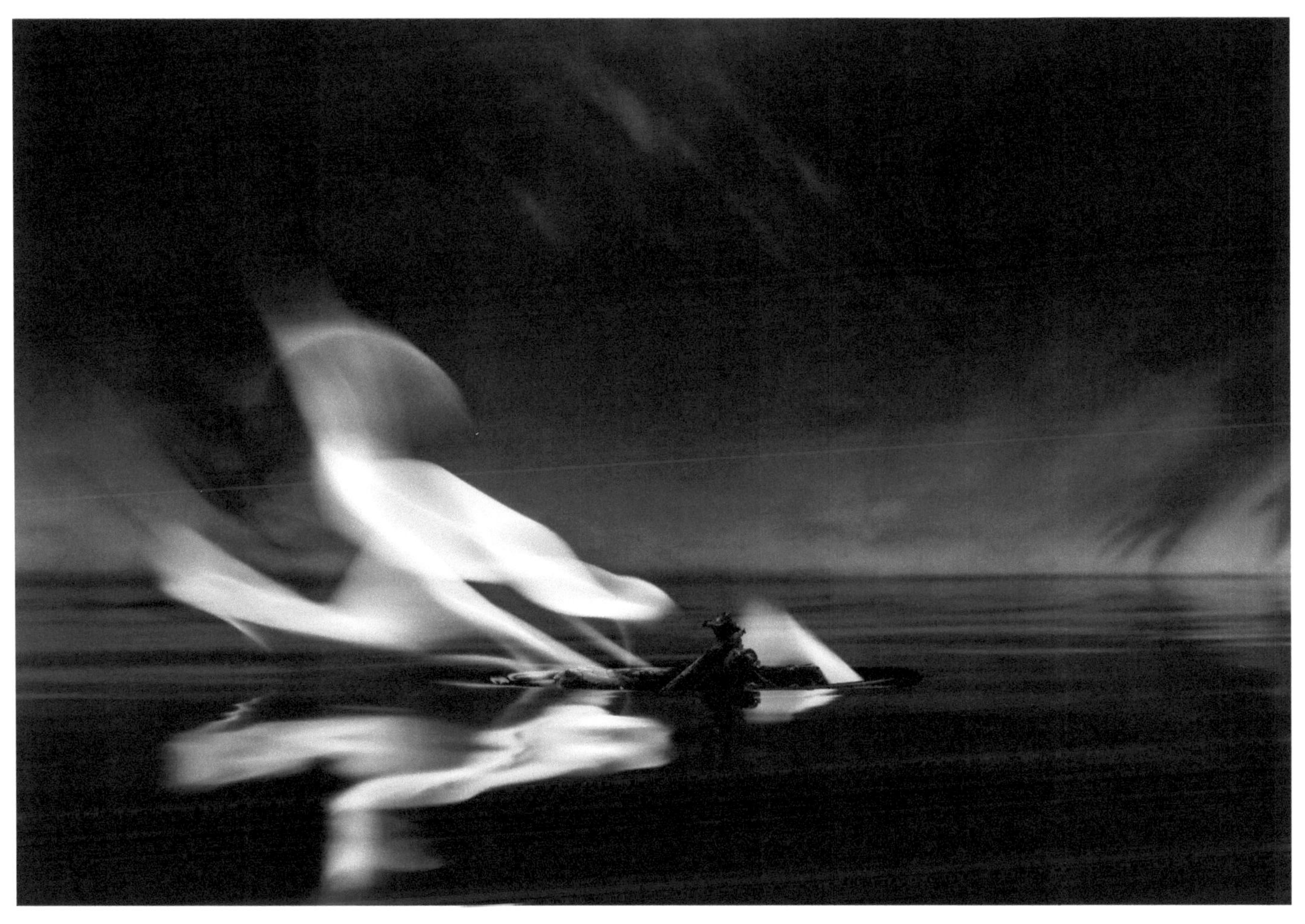

The Fall of Intention

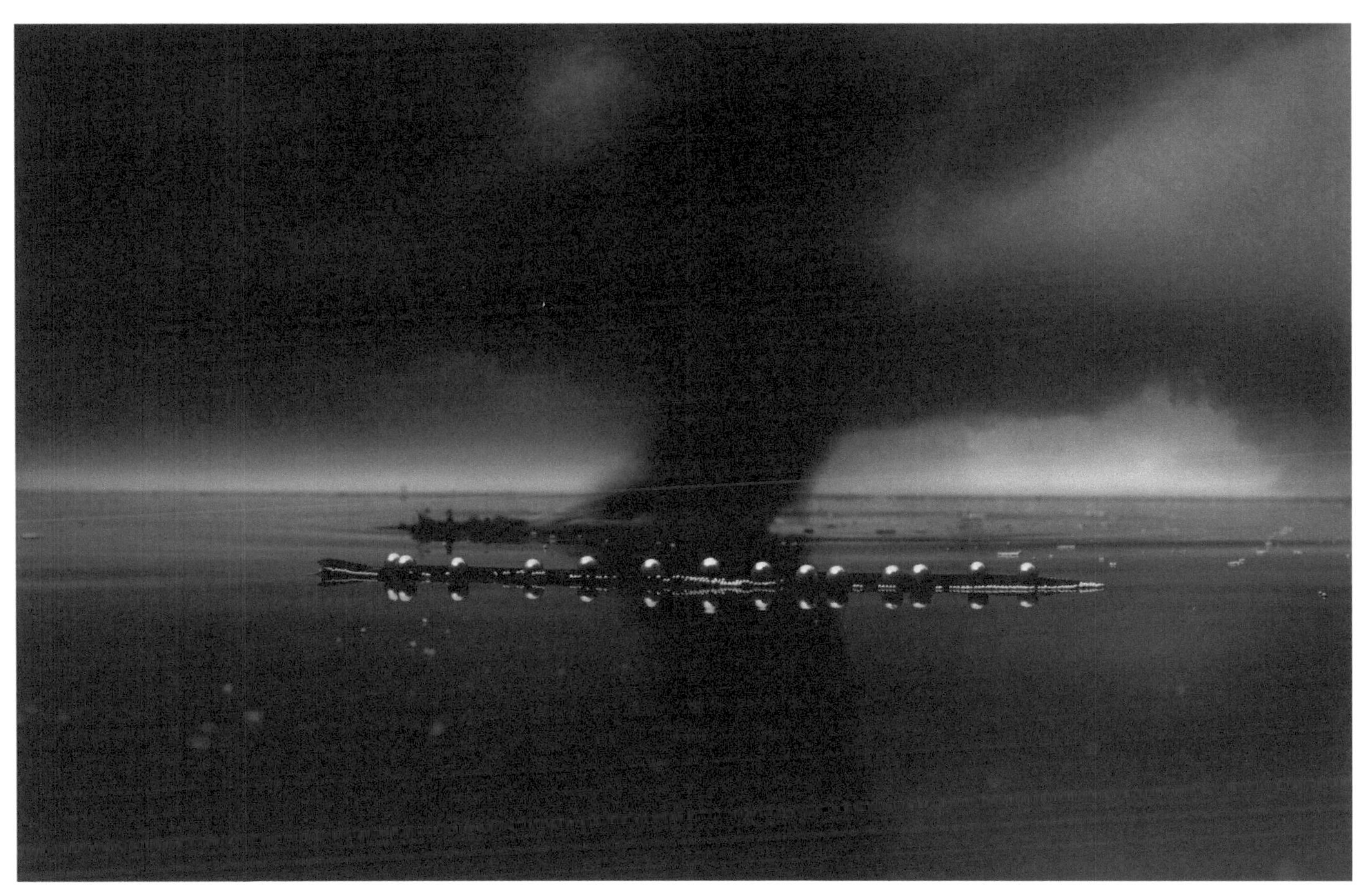

The Pearls of Shiva

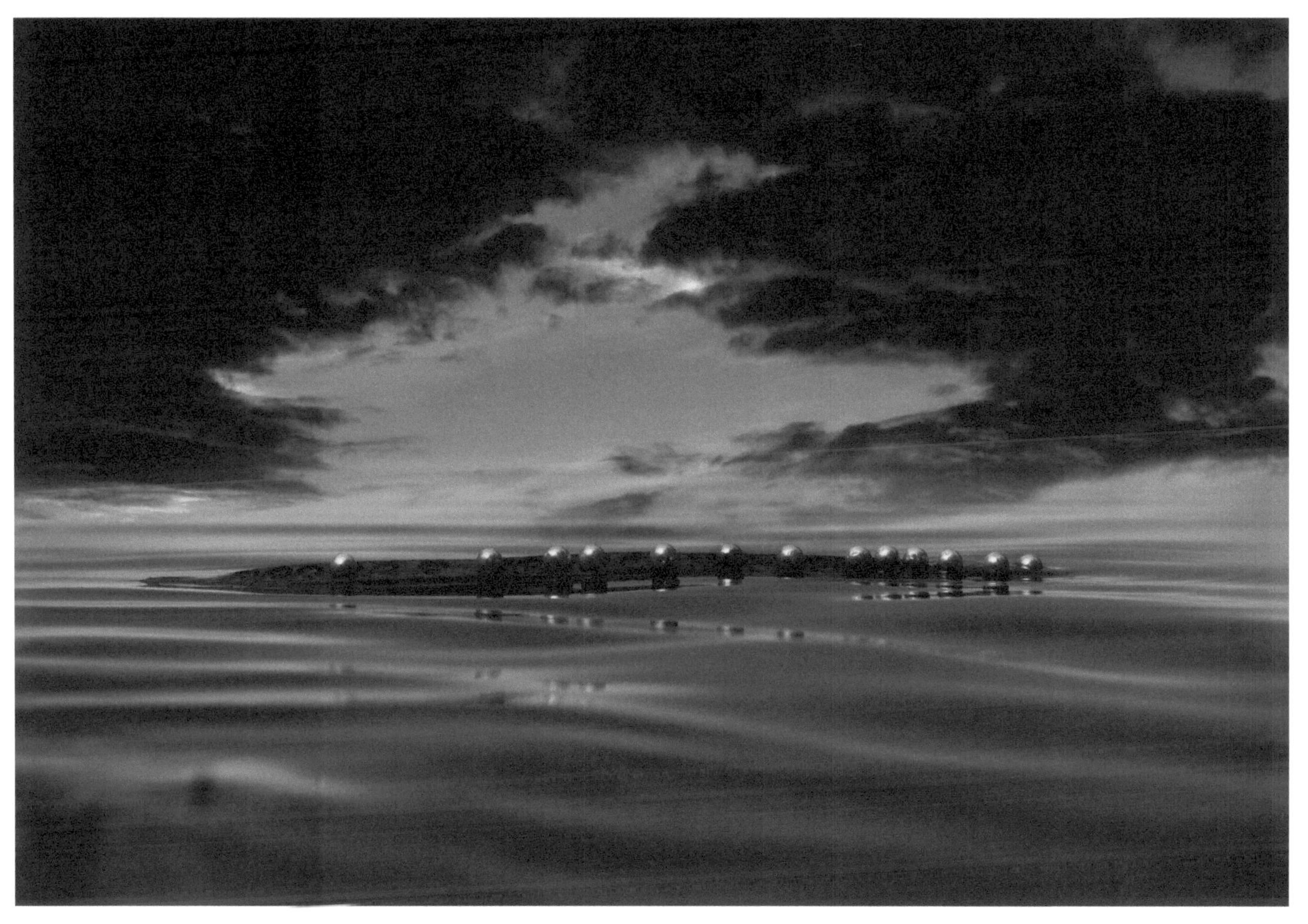

Raft of Pearls

Galen Garwood was born in 1944 and spent most of his young life growing up on St. Simon's Island, Georgia and Charleston, South Carolina. In 1966, after one year of art at University of Georgia in Athens, Georgia, he moved to Fairbanks, Alaska, where he majored in visual art and music with a miner in English. He moved to Seattle, Washington in 1971 and began exhibiting his paintings at Foster-White Gallery in 1973. Over the course of the last four decades, he has exhibited his paintings in the United States and in Europe. His creative contributions have also been expressed in writing, poetry, multi-media, and film.

In 1976 he won First Place in Painting at the Pacific Northwest Annual and in 1979, the Hassam Speicher Award at the Academy of Arts and Letters, New York, New York. His multi-media piece 'Adagio' won a Bronze Award at the International Multi-media Film Festival in Philadelphia, 1995, and in 1996 was included in the 1996 Venice Biennale's Xenograhia Nomadic Wall and again at 'Art Affair' in New York. His film 'Cadmium Red Light' received First Place for Narrative/Documentary at the Port Townsend International Film Festival in 2007 and a First Place Award for Short Documentary for 'Ed and Ed' at the DeReel Film Festival in Australia in 2008.

In 2006 he produced a short documentary on the work of American artist, John Franklin Koenig, and in 2007 a short documentary entitled 'Ed and Ed,' on the American painter Ed Cain and in 2008, another video documentary on the American ceramist, Anne Hirondelle.

Along with American poet, Sam Hamill, he created *Passport*, paintings and poems, published by Broken Moon Press in 1987 and the multi-media version in 1992, followed by *Mandala*, monotypes and poems, an Homage to Morris Graves, Milkweed Editions, 1993.

In 2011, he published a series of figurative photographs from Crete and Sicily, 1996, with poems by Peter Weltner entitled *The One-Winged Body* and the following year, 2012, again with Peter Weltner, paintings and poems, *Where Everything Is Water As Far As He Can See*, both published by Marrowstone Press.

He recently completed 'The Maenam Project,' a limited edition art book entitled *MAENAM, of Water, Of Light*, photographs with poems by Marvin Bell, James Broughton, Linda Gregg, Sam Hamill, Jeanne Morel, William O'Daly, Emily Warn, and Peter Weltner, Marrowstone Press, 2014.

A selection from his new series of photographs, 'Dream Sea,' is featured in a new book of poetry by William O'Daly, *The Road to Isla Negra*, published by Folded Word Press and in Peter Weltner's recent book of poems, *Water's Eye*, published by Marrowstone Press, 2015.

He lives in Northern Thailand.

www.ingramcontent.com/pod-product-compliance
Ingram Content Group UK Ltd.
Pitfield, Milton Keynes, MK11 3LW, UK
UKHW060116300726
14090UKWH00002B/220

* 9 7 8 0 6 1 5 6 6 6 3 9 6 *